MULTI-RACIAL SOUTH AFRICA:
THE RECONCILIATION OF FORCES

MULTI-RACIAL
SOUTH AFRICA

THE RECONCILIATION OF FORCES

Z. J. de BEER

Issued under the auspices of the
Institute of Race Relations, London

OXFORD UNIVERSITY PRESS

LONDON NEW YORK CAPE TOWN

1961

Oxford University Press, Amen House, London E.C.4

GLASGOW NEW YORK TORONTO MELBOURNE WELLINGTON
BOMBAY CALCUTTA MADRAS KARACHI KUALA LUMPUR
CAPE TOWN IBADAN NAIROBI ACCRA

Printed in Great Britain by Richard Clay and Company Ltd.,
Bungay, Suffolk

CONTENTS

INTRODUCTORY NOTE

BEFORE attempting to set forth the reasons why I believe that constitutional government in multi-racial South Africa can and must succeed I have studied the Institute of Race Relations' earlier publication: *South Africa: Two Views of Separate Development*. Those who have read that book will have been impressed with the cogency of the arguments both for and against the present government's policies. Mr. Pienaar, in support of separate development, argues that when the irresistible force of black nationalism meets the immovable object of white nationalism, there can be no peaceful solution other than the physical separation of the races; Mr. Sampson's reply, equally persuasively argued, is that the concept of separate development is quite impossible of achievement.

I do not write with the intention of refuting or replying to either of these writers; yet what I have to say will be more meaningful if read against the background of their work. For reasons which will become apparent to the reader, I am sure that in fifty or a hundred years' time South Africa will still be a multi-racial country. I am sure that white domination will not survive so long; I do not believe that partition on an effective scale will be achieved. Further, I have enough faith in our peoples to believe that, whatever troubles may have to be endured, they will not sink into chaos, but will find a system of government to which all South Africans can give allegiance. The why and the how of this belief form the subject matter of this book.

I

MEN AND FORCES

The course of politics is determined by the interaction of forces and men. Discernible in any society at any time are certain social forces, economic, psychological, demographic or what you will: forces which create pressures which determine the behaviour of people. In charge of affairs are men, men who must read these social forces and act in consonance with them. The man of affairs may be able to ride on the back of the social forces; he may be able to canalise and control them; he may, if he is strong, divert them; but seldom, if ever, can he stop them or drive them back.

In the old-established civilised countries of the world, it is generally true that the different social forces at work are seldom opposite in direction: indeed they tend more and more to pull together. Thirty years ago, for instance, management and labour in Western Europe still tended to believe that their interests were competitive, that more profit for management meant less pay for labour, and vice versa: today the lesson has been learnt that rising productivity is the key to the reconciliation of these traditionally opposing forces. It enables management to pay more and yet to enjoy the benefits of an expanding market, improved techniques and in turn more productivity. Today, the gap between a Capitalist and a Labour party in Western Europe is much smaller than it used to be.

The reconcilability of the social forces is thus one of the factors determining the stability of a country; but there is another very important factor. It is the extent to which the people themselves know and appreciate the value of order in a community and will voluntarily confine their political activities to constitutional or at any rate non-violent means. Here, too, the old democracies of the Western world have reached a stage of political maturity where only the most aggravated grievances will bring about insurrection. Generally speaking, the stability of these countries can be taken for granted.

It is not necessary to detail the instances in the post-war world where governments have proved unstable. It is sufficient to point out that in almost every case the requirements for stability have been absent: widely divergent social forces have been at work among people with little or no tradition of political maturity, and these forces, unchecked, have torn apart the societies in which they operate.

Where, judged by these criteria, does South Africa stand? Before considering our social forces, let us examine the political maturity of our people. It is difficult to measure this sort of quality with accuracy: perhaps the most illuminating method is comparison. In Western Europe, there is almost universal literacy; there is little poverty; the people, most of them, belong to religious bodies which preach non-violence and order; and there has been pretty advanced political organisation for very many years. It would seem fair to conclude that this is the sort of society that lends itself most easily to stable democratic government. By contrast, the failure of democratic government has been most complete in countries like Indonesia and, more recently, the Congo, where just the opposite conditions have applied: massive illiteracy, grinding poverty, primitive religious and cultural conditions and no tradition of government other than by domination.

On all these counts, the position of South Africa is intermediate. It is probable that half our people are literate. Wages paid to black South Africans, while very low by European standards, are so high by African ones as to attract men from all over Africa south of the equator. The Christian churches have done intensive missionary work for centuries, and well over half of our population are nominally Christians. Finally, very large numbers of our people have had some experience of democratic government at some level, and all of them have lived in an ordered society for a long time.

It is a tremendous mistake, therefore, though it is one often made, to equate the South African situation with that of any other African state. Nor is this merely true because the non-African population here is so very large. It is also true because the African in the Union is vastly more westernised in every way than his counterpart elsewhere. Viewed purely in terms of political maturity, the chances for the survival of parliamentary government in South Africa are not bad. They should indeed be the best on the continent of Africa. To the extent that parliamentary government is in danger—and there are many Jeremiahs to say it is—this is because of the centrifugal effects of the social forces that are at work. For the purposes of this chapter we shall examine these forces only briefly: they will be analysed in subsequent sections.

At a superficial glance, particularly from outside the Union, it may seem that the only forces of importance are white supremacy and black nationalism, and that they are exactly in opposition to each other and therefore irreconcilable. This is the premise on which many intelligent people outside South Africa found their pessimistic views, and it is also the sort of reasoning which has recently led many good South Africans to emigrate. But, on closer examination, it will be found that these two forces, while widely divergent, are not diametrically opposed, since each community is aware of its need for the other; and it is also demonstrable that there are other lesser but substantial forces which act in a direction intermediate between these two.

Our main argument will centre on the analysis of these forces, and in particular on an attempt to determine their composite effect. If there is to be successful parliamentary government in South Africa, then the line that it takes will have to approximate to the resultant of all the forces. It will of course not be possible to attune government to all these divergent forces at once. Indeed it may be that the right line is not really in tune with any of them. But if a real attempt is made to find the resultant force and follow it, then the forces pulling this way and that will be in balance with each other. Of course, even under these circumstances one population group or another might become so dissatisfied with the government as to repudiate its authority. It is here that the political maturity of the South African people becomes all-important. If the people understand the value of ordered government, and if it is manifest that a genuine attempt at fairness is being made, it seems reasonable to expect that unconstitutional resistance to government will be absent or at any rate minimal.

This may seem to be a rather theoretical argument, but it does show generally along what line the South African society will have to develop if it is to remain intact. If government follows the line of the resultant force, then the composite effect of the social forces will be, in general, to sustain it. But to the extent that government is out of line with that resultant, the social forces will warp or destroy government and chaos will result.

All this is only a way of repeating the profoundly true saying that government, if it is to succeed, must accord with the facts of power. Until the Second World War the Union of South Africa was pretty successfully governed, in the sense that law and order were maintained, nearly always by due process, the liberty of the subject was largely upheld and peaceful progress was made. This was so in spite of the fact that, by Western standards, the non-white peoples had woefully few rights or opportunities. It could be so, on our theory, because the real power of the non-white peoples was at that time also very limited indeed. Thus the will of the whites, measured in terms of power, was very nearly equivalent to the will of the people. This is now far from true. Industrialisation and education within the country, and developments in world circumstances and world opinion outside, have vastly increased the real power of the non-whites. There has been no corresponding alteration in the system of government; and consequently the signs of danger have appeared. More and more interference with the liberty of the subject has become necessary in order to maintain order; unrest and insurrection have begun to appear; and there are economic storm-clouds banking up. The system no longer accords with the facts of power. It must be made to do so; and there are few if any responsible groups in South Africa who have not in some way given recognition to this need. Some of the remedies offered will be examined, and an attempt made to prescribe the right one.

II

THE WHITE DYNAMIC:
AFRIKANER NATIONALISM

It has been observed that, up to the outbreak of World War II, non-white South Africans had little direct or indirect influence on the course of affairs. This is not to say that none of them played any part: on the contrary, there were many brilliant men of colour who were held in high esteem by the whites. Three were elected in mixed constituencies at different times to the Cape Provincial Council; and there were many men of real distinction on the Natives' Representative Council set up after 1936. Further, considerable attention was paid by successive governments to the wishes and wants of the non-whites. Yet our observation remains true. Politics were white politics; the political loyalties of the white voters were not much, if at all, influenced by their attitudes towards non-whites, while the non-white voters took their choice from among the white parties. The issues were those which divided white men one from another, very largely concerned with the Imperial factor, the relationship of South Africa to Britain and of English to Afrikaans-speaking citizens. Economics told too, of course; but only at times of crisis could economics overcome the Boer–British divisions.

In the first Parliament of 1910, Botha and Smuts led the South African Party majority, supported by nearly all the Afrikaners and the moderate English. The opposition was provided by the Unionist Party, who may be described as extremely pro-British. But the South African Party government did not remain intact for long. When Botha and Smuts appeared to go too far to appease the British, Hertzog broke away to lead the first Nationalist Party, committed to obtain a fair deal for the Afrikaner in South Africa and the constitutional freedom of South Africa in the world. This

Nationalist Party gained steadily at the expense of the South African Party, which was first forced to fuse with the Unionists in order to keep power and then defeated in 1924 by a coalition of the Nationalists and the Labour Party. In 1929 the Nationalists won an absolute majority. They remained firmly in power until the depression struck South Africa in the early thirties. In a time of real economic crisis, Hertzog and his followers went into coalition and then fusion with Smuts and the South African Party, forming the United Party. But, almost immediately, Dr. Malan led a small group out of fusion and formed what was known as the 'purified' Nationalist Party, which became once more the mouthpiece of Afrikaner aspirations. It gained strength rapidly during the thirties, and when Hertzog and Smuts broke apart at the outbreak of war in 1939, Hertzog rejoined Malan for a time in the Nationalist Party. The wartime period proved extremely difficult for the Nationalists, and in 1943 Smuts actually increased his majority on the war issue. But Dr. Malan was steadily rebuilding Afrikaner unity, and in 1948 he became Prime Minister. Since then the Nationalist Party has gained steadily in strength.

It is necessary to tell this story in order to show that over fifty years of Union Afrikaner nationalism has been the one irresistible force in our politics. Its only setbacks have been due to outside circumstances—an economic crisis and a war. Equally, however, it is necessary to realise what the source of this tremendous strength was. It was not, as many people outside South Africa tend to believe, built on colour prejudice. That came later, as we shall see. The Nationalist Party owed its formation and its growth to the aspirations of the Afrikaner people. In this field it has succeeded completely. The Nationalist victory in the republican referendum of 1960 has cleared the way for the realisation of its final ideal in the sphere of Afrikaner aspiration. From now on the Nationalists will stand or fall by their handling of the race problem in South Africa.

Of course, as the world knows, the race problem has been

in the forefront of our politics ever since the end of World
War II, and the Nationalist attitude to it is vitally important. None the less, it would be quite wrong to believe
that support for apartheid has been, even in the last fifteen
years, the binding force in the Nationalist Party. This has
been the concept of Afrikaner unity. And there is little
doubt that the strength of Afrikaner unity has served to
silence many who might otherwise have criticised apartheid.

To the world today, the name of the Nationalist Party is
virtually synonymous with the policy called apartheid.
Books can be and have been written on this subject; but for
present purposes a summary of its essentials is all that is
required. At the end of the war, the Nationalists saw that
there was a wave of liberal thought sweeping the world, and
that simultaneously the non-whites in South Africa were
rapidly being westernised and gaining real economic power.
They knew that a continuation of this state of affairs under
the Smuts government then in power would be likely to
lead to steady integration with growing influence for the
non-whites; and they shrewdly guessed that many white
South Africans would refuse to accept this prospect. On the
other hand, it would scarcely have been possible to campaign openly for a policy of naked repression: in any case,
many good and influential Nationalists would have refused
to do so on conscientious grounds. Therefore the idea of
apartheid, or separateness, was conceived. It is absolutely
essential to an understanding of the concept to realise that it
aims, in theory, at the attainment of full citizenship rights
by people of all races—but on a basis of geographical
partition. It is, or at any rate was, therefore possible for
people of impeccable moral standing to give support to it
as an idea, and many did so. As an election platform, it was
a brilliant success, for the white voter could support it in
order to protect his own sectional interests, and at the same
time assuage his conscience by believing that he was giving
the non-white a chance of real development in the future.
Even the Dutch Reformed Churches found it possible to

give it their blessing in 1950; but it must be noted that they only approved on condition that the separation really was territorially complete, and on a fair basis. Now that these conditions remain unfulfilled ten years later, the Church is changing its attitude, as we shall see.

Apartheid has failed utterly: of course it was always bound to do so, for two main reasons. First, if there was to be partition, there had to be adequate living space and economic opportunity for each community. To have provided these would have involved enormous sacrifices on the part of white South Africans, many of whom had supported apartheid for selfish reasons, and had no intention of paying for it. Second, the economy of all South Africa—industrial, mining and farming—depends upon a labour force which is at least eighty per cent black. To send these workers back to the reserves would cripple the economy: to keep them where they are and deny them rights is recognised as immoral even within the Nationalist Party. Officially, the Prime Minister and his followers cling to the line that apartheid will yet be worked out in practice. In fact, it may serve a little longer as a slogan, but as a policy it is finished. All that it has brought South Africa is internal unrest and external ignominy.

How, then, has this discredited policy retained for all these years the support of the mass of Afrikaans-speaking people, including ecclesiastical and academic leaders? Firstly and mainly, because it came from the nationalist movement and was therefore identified with the mystique of Afrikaner unity. Secondly, because most Afrikaans-speaking people are in a dreadful dilemma over the whole race question. They know that discrimination on grounds of race alone is impossible of justification: yet for a whole mass of historical and psychological reasons, the prospect of integration in a multi-racial society is repellent. In this conflict between conscience and instinct, apartheid appeared to provide a solution. As its failure becomes more apparent the choice will become more urgent.

B

The all-important question for the future, having regard
to the tremendous power of Afrikaner nationalism, is:
what are its minimum terms? What is it that the Afrikaner,
generally speaking, will insist upon having under any and
all circumstances? The answer that he would almost certainly give is: self-determination. The sense in which the
word is used here is, however, not precisely the same as its
general meaning. Self-determination to the Afrikaner does
not mean political independence as an isolated community.
It means the right to maintain the cultural heritage which
he has built up: his language, his religion, his way of life,
his economic standards. His fierce resistance years ago to
attempted anglicisation and his resistance today to the
extension of political power to non-whites flow from the
same deep-seated fear, natural enough in so small a people
with so turbulent a history. The fear is that he will lose his
dearly-bought identity. There are those who scoff at this
determination to keep it, who believe that the Afrikaner
will be swept aside easily by the course of events. They
should be reminded that others, particularly the British,
have from time to time in history made the costly mistake of
under-estimating the Afrikaner. No sensible plan for South
Africa should do this.

III

THE BLACK DYNAMIC: AFRICAN NATIONALISM

When South Africans discuss their country they frequently point out how different it is from any other. This may be irritating; but it is true. And because the country is different, African nationalism shows different characteristics in the Union from other territories.

First, the Union differs from other African territories in that for the most part it was not settled by Africans before the whites arrived at the Cape. Secondly, the whites are far more numerous and have been here far longer than is the case elsewhere. Thirdly, all the processes of civilisation referred to earlier have progressed much further here than elsewhere. Finally, the large and influential brown minorities play their moderating part in our political life. For all these reasons, African nationalism here has never been of the 'white-man-get-out' variety. Rather has it been a long and for the most part patient campaign by the black people for recognition as citizens in their own country. The aim of the African National Congress has always been a multi-racial South Africa rather than a black one.

As was inevitable, the last ten to fifteen years have seen a considerable 'hotting-up' of the whole process. For so long as it appeared that a gradual raising of the status of Africans and improvement of their conditions might be obtained by negotiation with the government, the African National Congress remained a most moderate body. But about the end of the war the gap between African aspirations and the concessions that the then government was prepared to make grew wider and relationships began to deteriorate. Since the Nationalists took office in 1948 the situation has, of course, gone from bad to worse. Various forms of non-violent demonstration have been conducted by the African

National Congress. On several occasions serious violence has broken out. The government and the police have adopted measures of increasing severity against these protests and indeed against African offences of every sort; and so the hostility has grown.

In spite of the increasing militancy of the movement, the African National Congress found two years ago that it could no longer satisfy all its followers. Its 'Young Turks' split off to form the Pan-Africanist Congress. This organisation adopted a tougher line than that of the African National Congress, and, as its name indicates, aligned itself far more closely with African nationalism generally. In particular it objected to the connexions the African National Congress had built up with certain non-African bodies which, the Pan-Africanist Congress alleged, were tainted with Communism. The young men of the Pan-Africanist Congress were in far more of a hurry than the more orthodox African National Congress leaders, and early in 1960 they launched what was to have been a nation-wide campaign against the pass laws. It was planned as non-violent, under the slogan 'No bail; no defence; no fine'; and it was planned to go on indefinitely until the pass law system was broken. The campaign turned out to be neither nation-wide nor non-violent: it led to the now notorious events of Sharpeville and Langa, to widespread disturbances throughout the country and to the declaration of a National Emergency that lasted for five months. While it seems clear that the African National Congress did not originally plan to participate in this campaign, they did eventually join in in some degree, and they certainly took their share of the punishment that was meted out.

Shortly after the Emergency was declared, the government introduced legislation for the permanent banning of both the African National Congress and the Pan-Africanist Congress. It was passed with the support of the United Party, and, officially at any rate, the two organisations then ceased to exist. Those who were imprisoned during the

Emergency included virtually all their leading members. They have since been released; but there is now no official organisation to be the mouthpiece of African nationalism.

That, however, does not mean that African nationalism does not still exist, or does not continue to have insistent demands. They are many; but three stand out clearly as the chief. First and foremost, the Africans demand the repeal of the pass laws—the system of regulations by which their freedom of movement is limited, their right to sell their labour restricted and their family life often interfered with. In this they have a large and growing body of white support. The churches, commerce and industry and many influential individuals have spoken out against these laws. The Progressive Party has come out squarely for repeal, while even the United Party urges substantial relaxation. During the height of the Emergency period the government actually raised hopes by suspending their effect for a while, but when they had the situation under control they reimposed the system. It does appear, however, that in some areas an effort is being made to ease its administration.

The second great African demand is for higher wages. Although wages are far better in the Union than elsewhere in Africa, they are still for the most part below the poverty datum line. Here, too, there is substantial support from commerce, industry, churches and the trade union movement, which is chiefly white. The government, while they have shown no anxiety to take any initiative in the matter, have no particular objection to the raising of wages, and some success is being achieved.

The third African demand, now general among the politically conscious elements, is for universal adult suffrage. It may be noted that this insistence on adult suffrage is of relatively recent origin, but that does not make it any easier to deal with. For this is something which the bulk of the Union's white population—and probably very many Coloureds and Indians—will simply not consider. These South Africans can often see that it is right and just, if

somewhat unpalatable to them, that Africans of proven
civilisation should share political power with them. They
can also see, many of them, that it is right and just and
necessary that all Africans should be given full educational
and economic opportunities. But what seems to them to be
wrong and unjust is the adoption of a technique of government which would subject them to the rule of relatively
uncivilised people. On the evidence of certain other states,
most notably the Congo, they believe that the grant of
universal adult suffrage in any African country would
simply place power in the hands of whatever demagogue
could most effectively arouse primitive emotions. Of course
it may be shown that the Congo and the Union are so
different that no parallel exists. Of course it may be pointed
out that in India and Nigeria largely illiterate electorates
are voting on a universal franchise, and so far the system is
working well. But the object of this work is not to argue the
theoretical merits of a system. It is to comment upon political
facts. And it is a political fact that, sooner than accept a
universal suffrage in present circumstances, white and
perhaps brown South Africans would turn to desperate
measures, for to them universal suffrage seems to spell the
end of their freedom and the end of their way of life.

What then of the African demand? Would the Africans
prove utterly unco-operative if offered anything less than a
universal suffrage? One does not know; but one does know
that their present apparent intransigence is in no small
measure a reaction to the intransigence of the present
government. An African leader can afford to counsel
moderation to his followers only if that moderation brings
dividends in the way of benefits. Where the moderate is
snubbed, the followers will naturally demand extreme
leadership: one might as well be hung for a sheep as a lamb.
Without labelling South Africa's present black leaders as
extremists, it is reasonable to suggest that this sort of process
has been taking place. As one African of substance put it
recently: 'Had General Smuts given us the vote in his life-

time we would have voted for him: today not one of us would support his policies.' Action and reaction are equal and opposite, and Newton's law often holds in politics too. White intransigence has bred black intransigence. In time perhaps we shall see whether white generosity will evoke an equally generous response.

IV

THE GROUPS BETWEEN

The English-Speaking Whites

The English-speaking whites in South Africa often complain that they are ignored and forgotten in politics. While this is an exaggeration, it is not without some truth: in the modern jargon, it might be said that they project no clear image. One of the best of their own poets, Anthony Delius, has written in his brilliant political satire *The Last Division*:

> These million English are a vague communion
> Indifferent to leadership or goal,
> Their most accomplished children flee the Union,
> Search other countries for their cause and soul,
> And to the pioneer premise of their fathers
> Add on no better moral, finer story,
> Leave our crude glaring sun and savage weathers
> To bask, reflect in other peoples' glory.
> Most able men, not all, who stay behind
> Fix loyalty to man upon shareholders,
> The other whites are voters of a kind
> And blacks are some statistics in their folders.
> Man may diminish while they make their pile,
> Black generations brew in new diseases,
> What if the legislation stinks of guile?
> What? If the supertax reduction pleases . . .
> Their language is looked after by the Jews,
> Their politics thought out by Afrikaners,
> Their colleges embalm enlightened views,
> While they get on with business and gymkhanas.[1]

---

[1] Anthony Delius, *The Last Division* (Human and Rousseau, Cape Town, 1959).

Delius' shafts are well aimed, if perhaps unnecessarily sharp. Certainly since Union, the greatest contribution of the English-speaking has been in the business sphere—and a very great contribution it has been.

Before judging the role of the English-speaking in politics, however, it would be well to remember the circumstances in which it has been played. As has been stressed, until very recently our politics were dominated by arguments between white people. English-speaking South Africans, by and large, were quite satisfied with the state of affairs just after Union, and wanted no more than to get on with the task of building the national economy within the British Empire. They genuinely could not understand why Hertzog and the Nationalists wanted to change things, and they resented them and their doings. They were in the minority, however, and had they allowed the struggle to become simply one of English versus Afrikaans, they must have lost rapidly. Very sensibly, therefore, they sought allies among those Afrikaners who shared their admiration for British institutions, and in the South African Party and later the United Party, they worked in hearty co-operation with them. Naturally, since the Afrikaans vote was in the majority, it was always necessary to woo Afrikaans voters; and naturally, therefore, the Afrikaner members of these parties tended to gain prominence. It is for this quite understandable reason, and not because of any inherent weakness, that they have always followed Afrikaner leaders—Botha, Smuts, Strauss, and now Graaff or Steytler.

It was shown earlier how, from 1948 onwards, the colour issue began to gain pre-eminence in our politics; and it is interesting to see how, once this happened, the loyalties of English-speaking voters began to alter. Just before the 1953 general election, the government's assault on the Cape Coloured franchise and the entrenched clauses of the Constitution roused them from their apathy. They joined the short-lived Torch Commando in huge numbers to protest, and went on to assist the United Party at the election.

Differences arose between the Torch and the United Party leaders, however, when the United Party voted in Parliament for certain punitive measures designed to suppress any potential rebelliousness among the Africans. Eventually, after the election, most of the Torch Commando in English-speaking Natal broke away to form the Federal Party, which stood for uncompromisingly pro-British policies and also, significantly, for a somewhat more liberal approach to colour matters. It flourished for a period, but has now lost virtually all its following. Almost at the same time there came into being the Liberal Party of South Africa, representing the viewpoint of complete non-racialism, and again including a number of disgruntled Torchmen who had either belonged to or supported the United Party. Though still active, it has never become strong. A year or so later, there was a further revolt in the United Party, this time a break-away of some of its most conservative members. There were some English-speaking men among them, but the Conservative Party they formed failed to draw support and soon died.

The United Party continued to command the loyalty of the vast majority of English-speaking voters until after the election of 1958. Another severe defeat was followed by another crisis, and this time, in August 1959, a more serious split occurred. Eleven United Party Members of Parliament resigned from the party, and, taking quite substantial numbers of party officials and members with them, founded the Progressive Party, committed to a non-discriminatory policy as between the racial groups which was, however, considerably more conservative than that of the Liberal Party. Just a year later this party tested its strength against the United Party in a Johannesburg suburb, and came within an ace of winning the by-election.

The Progressive Party resembles the United Party in that it is led by an Afrikaner, Dr. Jan Steytler, and has a fair number of Afrikaners among its leading members, but is composed mainly of English-speaking people. There is wide difference of opinion as to its prospects, but clearly it has drawn the support of a substantial part of the English vote, not this time on a basis of British sentiment but for a distinctive attitude to race relations. During the republican referendum campaign of 1960, when the issue was again largely one affecting the British connexion, the United Party, the Progressives, the Federals and most of the Liberals co-operated temporarily; but immediately after it they went their separate ways.

Now more than ever, with the republican issue settled, English South Africans have to think anew about their political viewpoints. And they have to do so in terms of race relations, for these are now the paramount issue. It would be rash to prophesy their attitude, and indeed it is improbable that they will act as a group in future. No one should make the mistake of thinking that all the English are well-disposed towards the non-whites, any more than all the Afrikaners are ill-disposed. Indeed, the most virulently reactionary views expressed in our politics have sometimes come from English-speaking men. Yet there are two factors which, generally speaking, distinguish them from their Afrikaans compatriots. Firstly, since nobody has ever interfered with the fundamental rights of English-speaking South Africans (as distinct from their sentimental loyalties, which have been repeatedly flouted), they have not the same fear of national extinction as have the Afrikaners. Secondly, while they are perfectly good South Africans, they naturally feel closer ties with Britain and the rest of the world than do Afrikaners, who have for historical reasons become more isolated. Therefore the English are on the one hand more susceptible to the liberalising influence of the outside world, and on the other hand more confident that they would have allies in time of need. For these reasons, and perhaps also because of their inherited British talent for compromise, they are on the whole likely to come to terms somehow with the aspirations of the non-whites. And time may show, when their fight is no longer merely a negative one in defence of the institutions they revere, that they have more talent for politics than many people now believe.

The Coloured Community

Between the hammer of white supremacy and the anvil of black nationalism live the two brown groups of South Africa, the Cape Coloured and the Asian (or Indian, as called here) communities. They have more in common than merely this misfortune, but on the other hand their political roles have been and may continue to be different.

The Cape Coloured people, a million and a half in number, have been called 'God's stepchildren'. It is really less than fair to charge the Almighty with responsibility in this way. Without doubt they are the children of God as we all are; but in the more earthly sense they are for the most part the descendants of white men and of the slaves and servants of white men. They have developed among the white people in the white man's towns and on his farms. They speak his languages, belong to his churches and share his tastes, from art to alcohol. To draw the line between Coloured people and whites is impossible, and the efforts of government officials to do so would be ridiculous if their effects were not so tragic.

Until relatively recent times, Coloured people in the Cape Province, where the vast majority live, were accorded substantially equal political and economic treatment with the whites; but since 1930 a succession of discriminatory measures has reduced their status further and further. In the other provinces it was always low. Yet, in spite of it all, the Coloureds have remained patient, generally law-abiding, good South Africans. Some of their intellectuals, despairing of any hope from the dominant whites, have tried to lead them into an alliance of protest with the Africans; but they have had little or no success. For culturally and in every way, the Coloured people belong with the whites; and they have stuck to them as an ill-used wife will often stick to her husband. But sooner or later, in the modern world, an ill-used wife will break free; and the whites should not make the dangerous assumption that the Coloureds will forever put up with discriminatory treatment. Happily, there are signs in both the Nationalist and United Parties that conservative white opinion is becoming aware of the need to improve the conditions of the Coloured people, and things may soon begin to get better.

There are, however, two mistakes that must be avoided. First, the politically conscious Coloured man is not asking for crumbs from the children's table: he wants equality of opportunity and the rights to which his citizenship entitles him. Therefore, whatever is done for the Coloured must be sufficient to be non-discriminatory. Secondly, many white men are inclined to believe that the proper strategy is to make the Coloureds the allies of the whites against the blacks. It is very doubtful indeed whether the Coloureds would accept so questionable a role; and if they did, South Africa would be worse rather than better off. The Coloured people can form a valuable bridge between black and white: it would be tragic if they were instead to become partisans in a struggle.

In terms of actual political attitudes, there is a vast range of views among the Coloured people. At one end of the scale are the militants who identify themselves closely with the African National Congress and indeed are often more uncompromising than the African leaders: at the other end there are some who are prepared to accept the apartheid structure, or most of it anyway. But probably it is fair to say that the solid bulk of Coloured people simply want to see political and economic opportunity on the same basis for all South Africans; they want increased opportunities for education and training; and they want their own rights as a minority group to be protected.

The Asians

As has been noted, the Asian group have much in common with the Coloured in that they, too, are a minority,

numbering only half a million; they are able, intelligent
people, some of whom have become very prosperous in the
face of great difficulties; and they are, in the main, a peaceful, law-abiding community. They have experienced in
Natal, where most of them live, bitter hostility from both
whites and Africans. Unlike the Coloureds, however, they
have a language and a religious and cultural background
of their own, and such affinity as they do feel for the
whites is based on economic rather than human considerations. Also unlike the Coloureds, they have never, for
practical purposes, enjoyed any worth-while political rights.
To a degree, though probably not to the extent that their
white detractors suggest, they are conscious of their link
with India and may look for support in that quarter; but it
should at the same time be emphasised that most of them
are South Africans of two or three generations, and that
they see their future here.

Politically, the division among the Indians is more clearly
marked than in the case of the Coloureds. The conservative section, representative largely of commercial interests,
aims at a solution by compromise with the whites, while the
larger though less affluent Indian National Congress is
closely associated with the African nationalist movement.

The Jewish Community

Normally, in a discussion of the groups making up the
South African population, one would not deal separately
with the Jewish community. Nor would they wish to be
regarded as separate in any way apart from religion. But
where one is discussing attitudes to race relations, it is a
fact that the Jewish people tend to have a distinctive
approach. It is also true that they are influential in many
spheres of South African life, and must be counted as one of
the forces in the South African situation.

For historical reasons, Jews are better aware than anyone
else of the ghastly dangers of racialism. They realise, as
many other white South Africans do not, that discrimina-

tion not only frustrates its victim but corrupts its instigator. For this reason, while there are many Jews in the United Party and even a few among the Nationalists, it may be said that the political centre of gravity of the community as a whole tends towards non-discriminatory policies, and that their influence will be exerted in that direction.

In this and the preceding chapters, the political attitudes of South Africans have been analysed on a group basis. Of course there are pitfalls in doing this, for, thank Heaven, South Africans are individuals just as other people are, and group conformism in politics is by no means the invariable rule. None the less, the awkward fact has to be faced that these groups do exist. Indeed, the South African dilemma stems from this fact. Group attitudes and group loyalties are among the forces which have to be reconciled if our society is to survive and prosper.

V

ECONOMIC FORCES

There are those who contend that the whole history of modern countries has been and will continue to be dictated by economics. There are others who believe that this is dangerous over-simplification; and certainly in South Africa human and psychological factors play an extremely important part. Nevertheless, it can be shown that many of the events of our history, and in particular many of the major developments in race relations, were the direct result of economic needs. Indeed it is arguable that the white South African who today complains so bitterly of the complexity and difficulty of the racial situation has only himself to blame, for his involvement with the non-white races today has come about by his own wish and decision, with the profit motive always present.

Long, long ago the early Dutch settlers found the Hottentots and Bushmen an unreliable labour force: so they imported slaves, who provided the stock of today's Coloured population. Much later, the English settlers in Natal found the Zulus unsuitable for work in the cane plantations: so they imported Indian labourers, and today their descendants complain about the 'Indian problem'. Later still, the gold mines of the Transvaal required labour, and Chinese were brought in. Most of these were repatriated as a result of public outcry, but some of their descendants remain, a half-forgotten group hovering between the whites and the non-whites and occasioning headaches for the busy men who classify races.

As against this, it is of course true that the white man did not import the black African. He did not; but he did quite deliberately entice and almost force the African to leave his kraal and come to work on the farms and in the towns. At one time, when the gold mines were crying out for labour,

it was found difficult to persuade the African to come to
work in them. The government accordingly increased taxa-
tion, not so much because the revenue was required as with
the deliberate aim of forcing the men to come to work to
earn a cash wage so as to pay the tax. This was successful. In
addition, of course, the mines themselves, with government
approval, set up a vast organisation to recruit labour not
only from the Union's Native Reserves but also from neigh-
bouring countries as far away as Tanganyika. This last is
the reason for what is known as the 'foreign Bantu problem'.

All these facts are only illustrations of what is really the
strongest, most continuous trend in South African history:
the economic integration of black with white in the building
up of the strongest, most diversified economy on the continent of Africa. And this is what makes nonsense—day by
day greater nonsense—of the apartheid policy. The pattern
held out as the end-aim of apartheid, with the Africans
living in their own territories and only leaving them temporarily, is more or less the situation that obtained a
hundred years ago. Since then South Africa has moved
further and further away from it. Most striking of all is the
fact that the past twelve years of government dedicated to
apartheid have scarcely slowed this integration, let alone
reversed it. The 1960 census reveals enormously increased
black populations in the so-called 'white' towns, and these
figures show quite clearly that all Dr. Verwoerd's horses and
all his men have no hope whatever against the mighty force
which drives black and white South Africans together to
earn their living.

Few things are more certain than that this inter-
dependence and therefore this integration will continue.
Prosperity accelerates economic integration, recession slows
it down, but no production on any scale is possible without
it. Whatever solutions we South Africans find for our problems must take account of this fact. In most societies
economic integration, placing economic power in the hands
of the working classes, would lead inevitably to the organised

C

use of that power to obtain better living standards and political power. Sooner or later, no doubt, this would happen in South Africa; but up to now it is happening only very slowly, if at all. The reason for this, stated shortly, is that the mass of the workers belong to a different community from their employers, and are subject to restrictions which deprive them of many of the weapons which workers elsewhere have at their disposal. It is also probably fair to say that the African is not temperamentally very well suited to the sort of organisation which is usually involved in such processes.

What is extremely interesting, and may prove to be very significant, is that in this situation the initiative to improve workers' conditions is beginning to come from their employers. A hundred or even fifty years ago this would have been an exceptional thing, but in the modern world with its modern economic concepts it is in fact not strange at all. In recent years it has been observed by industrial management that productivity has risen little if at all in South Africa while it has gone up by leaps and bounds in other industrial countries. Three main reasons have been adduced to account for this. First, lack of confidence in the government's race policies has inhibited investment, both local and from overseas, to a degree that has prevented the introduction of new techniques and equipment. Second, the restrictions which govern the conditions under which Africans work and limit their freedom of movement have the overall effect of making most of them impermanent and unstable employees, with obvious adverse effects on skill and productivity.

The third reason is the most interesting of all. In other industrial countries, a steady rise in wages has, of course, produced a steady growth in the internal market, with the result that management, producing on an ever-growing scale, has been able to reduce unit costs and increase productivity. In South Africa, the low wages earned by so many workers virtually exclude them as purchasers of any but the most elementary human requirements, with the result that industry cannot expand its scale of production as it would wish. The perception of this fact, together with a genuine altruistic desire to improve standards of living, has led to a strong move by industrial and commercial management towards higher minimum wages. Classically, of course, it has always been held that to increase wages without at least an equal rise in productivity is to invite inflation. Even this maxim is queried in South Africa, for it is argued that the very cheapness of labour tempts management to use it in an inefficient way, so that a rise in wages could and would be met quickly by improved production techniques. Further, some industrialists at least believe that the depressed conditions in which many workers live exert a directly depressing effect on individual productivity, which would immediately respond to an improvement. For these reasons, highly responsible and experienced businessmen in the Union believe that the proper course is to raise wages without waiting for a prior rise in productivity.

Of course, rising wages and improved techniques often result in a sharp reduction of the numbers of people employed by a particular industry. In suitable circumstances at any rate, this slack is soon taken up because the increased buying-power of the higher-paid workers creates additional demand for the services of those who have become redundant. But in the particular circumstances of South Africa, it is not necessary to rely on this, for South Africa employs very large numbers indeed of non-Union Africans who come to work in the mines and to some extent in other spheres. Since these workers send or take a good deal of their pay home, they are of relatively less value as consumers in the Union's economy. If then raised efficiency were to lead to reduced employment opportunities—and it is by no means certain that in the overall picture it would do so— this could still take place at no cost at all and probably with benefit to the Union's economy.

There is one other factor of importance in assessing our

economic needs: the question of external markets, particularly for manufactured goods. It has become almost trite
to say that South Africa should be the workshop of the
African continent. To a degree of course she is, but not
nearly to the extent that she could normally expect. And
there can be no doubt that a powerful reason for this dis-
appointing state of affairs is the purely political one. People,
particularly black people, elsewhere have developed an
animosity towards South Africa which in turn causes
definite sales resistance, and which is closing markets to us.
It is not so much the organised consumer boycotts that
harm us as the spontaneous resistance that our goods are
beginning to encounter. A dramatic instance of the harm
we are suffering is provided by a South African manu-
facturer who, finding it impossible to market his product in
West Africa, has purchased a factory in the United King-
dom in order to make the identical article for export back to
Africa. The loss to South Africa is obvious.

For purely economic reasons, then, there is a powerful
incentive to change present policy in a number of ways and
to do things which are normally suspect in South Africa as
'liberal'. Since the interests which are pressing for these
changes are not normally active in politics, this trend may
validly be regarded as another force shaping our political
destiny at this time.

VI

NATIONAL INSTITUTIONS

In these days when press and radio carry news and views so rapidly to so many people, any person or body of persons regarded as newsworthy can influence public opinion and therefore the politicians. Indeed the process is often short-circuited in that the politician keeps his own ear attuned to what is said. And it is well recognised that whenever a representative organisation holds a conference or meeting, it may and usually does issue a statement of its findings which is carried by the press into virtually every literate home in the country. This technique has been widely employed in South Africa recently, and there can be little doubt that it will play some part in the shaping of events.

Traditionally in South Africa, people who were not themselves active politicians were reluctant to speak about the thorny subject. Certainly churches, universities and businessmen, whether individually or collectively, observed a pretty strict rule in this regard. As the failure of present policies has become more apparent, however, all these and other bodies have felt compelled to come forward with public statements of their views, and during most of 1960 there was a spate of such declarations.

The Churches

Back in 1948, when apartheid first came into the limelight, the obvious religious questions were raised and debated. In particular, the Dutch Reformed Churches were challenged as Christian bodies to say whether or not they approved of adverse discrimination on grounds of race. Now what these Churches say on a national matter is of absolutely vital importance. For the Dutch Reformed Churches and the Nationalist Party consist very largely of the same people,

and the Afrikaner people are, by and large, good church-
goers who respect the views of their pastors. This is not to
say—and in fairness this should be emphasised—that the
Church is in any sense the tool of the party. The Anglican
priest here who adapted a well-known dictum and described
the Dutch Reformed Church as the Nationalist Party at
prayer did no one, least of all himself, a service. What is true
is that the Dutch Reformed Church has played a vital role in
the whole Afrikaner movement, in building the Afrikaner
people from the backward, depressed, defeated community
that they once were to the vigorous group that they are
today. It has been said: '*Jy kan nie die Afrikaner sonder sy
Kerk verklaar nie*' (You cannot account for the Afrikaner
without his Church).

In 1950 the Dutch Reformed Churches met in a special
congress to discuss the question of the apartheid policy.
They found in favour of it, but on strict and circumscribed
terms. They did not in any way justify adverse discrimination on grounds of race. What they advocated was a strict
and total partition, with no blacks in the white areas or vice
versa. Recognising to some extent the economic problems
this involved, they called for large-scale unskilled white
immigration to fill the jobs now held by black men, and envisaged very heavy investment to build up a separate
economy in the black areas. Of course this scheme was never
practical politics, and Dr. Malan, then Prime Minister,
said so at the time. Further, it would be naïve to deny
that many of those at the congress were influenced by a
desire to find a formula which would be acceptable to the
Nationalist Party as well as to the Church. None the less,
the Church remained true to Christian principles in what it
enunciated.

The other main churches in South Africa never did support the apartheid idea. Most of them, however, remained
relatively silent about it for years, partly from a wish to
keep out of politics and partly in order to give the policy a
fair chance. But as time went by the restrictive edifice of

apartheid laws was built up with precious little sign of any positive development of the Native areas. It became obvious that real injustice was being caused, and one by one church leaders began to speak out in condemnation of the policy being applied. Almost all the churches other than the Dutch Reformed Church have condemned apartheid, and they have done so in very clear terms. They have borne witness to the great principle that all men are equal before God, and that therefore no race discrimination whatever can be justified.

This wide difference of approach between the Dutch Reformed Church and the other churches has led, as might have been expected, to considerable strain and even from time to time to open recrimination. Eventually, in 1960, a meeting of the World Council of Churches was held in Johannesburg. The Dutch Reformed Churches were well, though not fully, represented; and the representatives of the largest Dutch Reformed Churches' organisations gave support to the resolutions taken. These were of such a kind as to cause a real crisis within the Church and within the Nationalist Party. The Dutch Reformed Church delegates concerned still proclaimed their faith in a policy of territorial segregation so far as this might be possible; but they came out firmly in opposition to any discrimination against those non-whites who live permanently outside the African territories. At the same time they utterly condemned the concept of migrant labour. Taken together, these resolutions strike at the very heart of the apartheid policy as it is being applied. As this is being written, there is no clear information as to what percentage of the Dutch Reformed Church membership will support this viewpoint; all that can be said is that, for the first time, a large and influential section of the Dutch Reformed Church leadership has condemned vitally important aspects of government policy. The strength of church criticism of the government is now very formidable indeed.

The Universities

In the universities of South Africa the situation and its development are very similar. After 1948 it could be said that the Afrikaans-medium universities were solidly behind the government and the English-speaking ones against it. Largely, the universities tried to keep out of party politics. Certain Nationalist intellectuals, mainly identified with a body called SABRA (South African Bureau for Racial Affairs), gave very strong support to the apartheid ideology; but, as with the Dutch Reformed Church, this was on the basis that it would be complete partition. As this has failed to materialise many of these men have become increasingly disillusioned with the Nationalist Party, and while they have not as yet found another party to support there is a more or less open breach between the SABRA leaders and the government. As to the English-medium institutions, whatever reluctance there had been to enter the political field vanished with the government's introduction of a policy of forced racial segregation at the universities. The utter condemnation of government policy in these circles is now virtually unanimous.

Commerce and Industry

While churches and universities in South Africa are more or less evenly divided on Afrikaans–English lines, the same is not true of business organisations. It is true—and unfortunate—that Nationalist-minded Afrikaner businessmen have formed their own representative institutions in both commerce and industry; but these are very small and unimportant compared with the Associated Chamber of Commerce and the Federated Chamber of Industries. These latter two organisations are the main mouthpieces of the economic leaders of South Africa. For a long time after the Nationalists came to power these bodies were markedly reluctant to offer any criticism of government policy, although quite often independent economists demonstrated good grounds for doing so. Their reluctance to criticise the government stemmed largely from the old-established habit of 'staying out of politics', and also from the facts that there were boom conditions for the first seven or eight years of Nationalist rule, and that the Nationalists took a good deal of trouble to help commerce and industry in a technical way. Gradually, however, it became apparent that the greatest departmental exertions by the government were insufficient to offset the effects of diminished investment due to lack of confidence in their race policies, that the application of pass laws, influx control and later job reservation was seriously impairing the labour situation, and that the country was suffering from an unsatisfied need for skilled immigrants. This last was due initially to Nationalist opposition to immigration, and later, when the government changed its attitude, to the reluctance of potential immigrants to come to a country with obvious racial problems. On all these and other counts commerce and industry became more and more critical as time went on, and by the end of 1959 were sharply so. Then the disturbances of 1960 occurred, causing the greatest alarm not only in South Africa, but among her friends and all those who did business with her. A rapid flight of capital took place, causing balance-of-payments problems and raising the prospect of control measures harmful to the internal economy.

Alarmed by all this, and also genuinely saddened by the occurrences in the Union, our businessmen spoke out clearly and repeatedly, individually and collectively. Among the most striking pronouncements was the considered statement of the Association of Chambers of Commerce, issued in May 1960. Declaring frankly that the economy was in jeopardy and that they felt it their duty to make their views public, they went on to demand freedom of economic opportunity for all South Africans, radical amendment if not repeal of the pass law-influx control system, the admission of Africans to trade unions and other far-reaching reforms. The views of Assocom were echoed in varying degree in

dozens of other statements from the business world. Even
some of the Afrikaans business organisations associated
themselves with the milder criticisms, and certainly they did
not rush to the defence of the government.

In striking agreement with the views of these employer
organisations have been those expressed by employees
through their main organisation, the Trades Union Council.
Joining in the spate of pronouncements on the crisis situation in 1960, the Trades Union Council presented a
memorandum to the government's economic advisory
council in July. In it they pressed for a national minimum
wage, for the right of Africans to join trade unions, for the
entrenchment of the principle of equal pay for equal work
for the different races and, perhaps most significant of all,
for the replacement of the pass laws by a simple identity-
card system. This expression of view is particularly im-
pressive when one considers that it comes from the white
workers—the very people who, superficially, have most to
fear from non-white competition. The fact that the unions,
which at one time in South Africa were bastions of white
privilege, have come to this point of view is partly due to
their perception of the economic realities, partly to the
inspiration of a leadership which genuinely believes in the
old Labour concept of the brotherhood of man. While
organised labour in South Africa is nothing like the political
force that it is in other countries, it can still be significant.
The former Labour Party has virtually disappeared: the
unions are fundamentally at odds with the Nationalists and
display no great enthusiasm for the United Party. In terms
of policy, the Trades Union Council would appear to have
much in common with the Progressive Party, but whether
they will in fact give it support remains to be seen.

The Press

It would be wrong to conclude this chapter without
reference to the press itself, in most countries a most potent
instrument in the formation of public opinion. It is an odd

fact that in South Africa, though the Afrikaans-speaking white population is almost twice as large as the English-speaking, the combined circulation of English newspapers appears to be about four times that of Afrikaans ones. There is no evidence, however, that their political influence is in proportion. Virtually the whole of the Afrikaans press, at any rate the politically conscious journals, is tightly linked to the Nationalist Party. Again, the whole of the English press, while quite independent of any party, is strongly hostile to the government. In general, it may fairly be said that the English press goes a good deal further than the official opposition, the United Party, in opposing Nationalist philosophy and policies. Since the emergence of the Progressive Party, most English papers have taken up an editorial position somewhere between these two groups; but it is possible that it is only realistic uncertainty about the political strength of the Progressives that prevents their having whole-hearted support from most of the papers.

The Afrikaans papers, all of them, were for many years the tireless propaganda instruments of the Nationalist Party. Only in recent years has an occasional critical note been heard from some of the more strong-minded editors; and then it is criticism 'in the family', as it were. In the last months of 1960, however, the most distinguished and probably most influential of all the Nationalist papers became so critical as almost to challenge the government. This was *Die Burger*, of Cape Town, the organ of the Nationalist Party in the Cape, thought to have close links with the SABRA intellectuals and the more liberal elements in the Dutch Reformed Church. It certainly did not urge any actual defection from the Nationalist Party; but it was prepared to highlight the divisions which there are within the party in an attempt to force some liberalisation of policy.

This does not exhaust the list of influential organisations in the Union. Most others, however, notably the powerful agricultural unions, have continued to avoid taking up political attitudes. It appears from the review presented here that there is a strong and almost uniform trend towards more political participation and more criticism of Nationalist policies. But as yet there is no evidence that this has even begun to sap the political power of the Nationalist Party. The Nationalists wield their two weapons of Afrikaner sentiment and white prejudice so effectively that up to the present they have succeeded in keeping the votes even of many of their critics. It must be doubtful, however, whether this position can be maintained indefinitely.

VII

THE WORLD OUTSIDE

It has already been observed that, by returning a Nationalist government in 1948, South Africa turned towards racialism at the very moment when the whole world was moving against it with more determination than ever before. It is scarcely surprising, then, that our popularity outside our own borders has waned as rapidly as it has. But it is unfair for critics of the Nationalists to suggest that they alone are responsible for this. Already in 1947 the far more benevolent 'White Leadership with Justice' policy of General Smuts had been under heavy fire at the United Nations; and no realist can doubt that the continuation even of that policy until today would have involved us in great and growing outside criticism—not so much because it was wrong in its time, but because it would now be quite out of date. Probably, of course, had Smuts and Hofmeyr remained in command, South African policy would have moved with the times; but this is purely hypothetical. The fact of the matter is that the chorus of world criticism which reached a crescendo in 1960 after the Sharpeville and Langa shootings is directed not purely at the Nationalist government but at the whole concept of race discrimination. In attempting to assess present political history in South Africa, one must ask what pressures are likely to be exerted from outside in expression of this criticism, what their effect is likely to be and what would have to be done to check them.

The Commonwealth

Historically, and in some degree even today, South Africa's relations with the rest of the world are dominated by her membership of the Commonwealth of Nations.[1] The

[1] See Postscript, page 69.

influence of the Commonwealth over the Union has of course declined steadily over the past fifty years, partly because of the changing character of the Commonwealth itself and partly because of the increasingly assertive character of South African nationalism—nationalism in a sense which includes but is not confined to that of the Nationalist Party.

Attitudes in the Union towards the Commonwealth vary widely. Among the English-speaking there are many who simply favour the maintenance of the closest possible tie with Britain. Then there are those who, though not particularly pro-British, believe fervently in the Commonwealth as a bastion of Western values and an instrument of inter-racial co-operation. Thirdly there are those, including many Nationalists, who, while rejecting the idea that Commonwealth opinions should be allowed to influence South African politics, favour maintenance of the Commonwealth link for the sake of the concrete benefits that it brings. And finally the extreme Nationalist group, whose size is difficult to estimate, presses on largely sentimental grounds for the final 'cutting of the painter'. Non-white opinion on this matter is difficult to assess. Many of the most cynical and disillusioned among them refuse to see any importance in the Commonwealth link, regarding it as in any case too weak to offer them any real hope. Some even go so far as to hope that it will be broken, believing that this will hasten the disintegration of the South African society which to them spells repression and denial of opportunity. These, however, are the symptoms of frustration. In general, there can be little doubt that non-white South Africans would favour our continued membership of an organisation which is firmly opposed to race discrimination. Overall, then, there can be little doubt that South Africans desire by a large majority to retain membership if possible.

The whole question of Commonwealth membership has been thrown into sharp relief by the holding of the referendum campaign which gave the government a mandate to declare a republic in South Africa. The mistake that many South Africans make, however, is to believe that others in the Commonwealth are primarily concerned with whether we are a monarchy or a republic. This is not so: responsible opinion everywhere concedes that the form of government in the Union is a matter for her own citizens to decide. It is the Union's race policy that matters, and the republic is only important because it presents the other members of the Commonwealth with a choice whether or not to expel us— or, to put it correctly, whether or not to renew our membership.

This has placed them on the horns of a dilemma: on the one hand, Commonwealth leaders realise that, as long as we remain 'in', the threat of expulsion is a lever that can be used to influence our policy towards the acceptance of Western standards. On the other hand, a threat too long suspended loses its effect, and many are wondering whether the time has not come to leave South Africa to her own devices.

If South Africa goes out of the Commonwealth, then such influence as the Commonwealth may have over her policies will clearly disappear; indeed it is possible that there will be a further reaction away from Commonwealth ideals. If South Africa remains in, it is important to consider what pressures, other than the threat of expulsion, the Commonwealth might apply, and what their effect might be. Certain attempts have been made to influence South African policy, with different results. There was the movement in Britain to organise a consumer boycott of South African goods. Not only was this not successful from the quantitative point of view: there is little doubt that it evoked a psychological reaction in South Africa entirely opposite to the effect it was intended to create. Psychologically, we South Africans react very differently to, say, disinvestment by British financial interests and boycott movements of this type. The one we see as reflecting genuine lack of confidence in our policies on the part of objective, if not always correctly informed, persons of experience. The other we tend to see as an attempt to damage us for purely political motives. Theoretically, of course, really large-scale boycotts could virtually paralyse South Africa; but if South Africa did capitulate to them it would be a sullen surrender after a bitter struggle—not the voluntary move towards a better policy which is presumably hoped for.

Quite apart from economic pressures, our sister Commonwealth nations can and do exert a purely moral pressure by their comments on our policies and their attitudes towards us in world affairs. Here again, psychological factors determine the effectiveness or otherwise of the pressure. If it seems to South Africans that the speaker is simply striking a pose for the edification of others, and has no real feeling of sympathy for us, then his criticism is likely to be rejected with contumely. If however we are persuaded that he is a real friend who wishes to help, the reaction will be quite different. An outstanding example of the correct psychological approach was the visit of the British Prime Minister early in 1960. During a stay of some weeks in our country he made his friendship perfectly obvious to us. Then, on the eve of his departure, he delivered his celebrated 'wind of change' speech. Even in the speech itself, he eschewed anything that savoured of nosey-parker criticism. He again emphasised the wish of his people to be friendly and helpful, and then showed that they could only continue in this role if South Africa abandoned racial discrimination in her own policies. Mr. Macmillan was, it is true, attacked by reactionary elements in both the Nationalist and United Parties; but in the main his speech had a positive effect on thinking South Africans.

The United States of America

Naturally, the Commonwealth nations are not the only ones whose opinions are important to South Africans. Attention is given in varying degree to views expressed in all Western countries, and for obvious reasons the United

States of America is particularly important. Here again, the effect of what is said or done depends largely on whether the criticism seems to us to be friendly or hostile, genuinely helpful or simply posturing for ulterior motives. When, for example, Mr. Charles Engelhard, an American financier who has acquired large interests in South Africa and urged others to do so, gives warning that our policies are making capital for investment in South Africa very difficult to obtain, he is listened to with respect. When, on the other hand, the President-elect says in general terms that it is his policy to support African nationalism, South Africans react adversely, not merely because they are themselves opposed to many of the aims of that movement, but because they feel that, having regard to the attitudes of at any rate some of its leaders, this must be an ill-considered statement; and because the ulterior motive for making it is all too obvious.

The United Nations

The question of South Africa's relationship to the United Nations organisation is a very wide and complicated one. South Africans have realised from the beginning that the conflict between the aims of the U.N. and our own policies was bound to make us the target of attack. None the less, with one brief intermission the government has consistently rejected the call from some of its own hot-headed supporters to ignore the U.N. It has been a consistent attender and has constantly put its own case. South Africa has relied heavily on the clause in the charter prohibiting interference in the internal affairs of member nations, and on the whole with success. Recently, however, two potential breaches in this defence have appeared. One breach was made shortly after Sharpeville and Langa, when the Security Council, acting presumably in terms of its own power to interfere where there is a threat to world peace, instructed the Secretary-General to enter into consultation with the South African government about its policies. Nothing has so far come of this, and it must be somewhat doubtful whether anything

D

will; but in due course there will presumably have to be a
report back, with possible consequences.

The second potential breach in South Africa's defence
concerns the position of the mandated territory of South
West Africa. Broadly speaking, the United Nations
organisation contends that it has inherited from the League
of Nations powers of supervision over the administration of
the territory: the South African government refuses to
accept this. Towards the end of 1960 a virtually unanimous
resolution of the General Assembly presented what was in
effect an ultimatum to South Africa either to change her
policy in South-West or to relinquish the mandate. That this
creates an extremely delicate situation is fully understood in
the Union and most particularly in South-West itself; and
further developments may have a profound effect on our
foreign relations and even conceivably on our internal
policy.

The Effects of External Pressures

After this by no means exhaustive review of external
pressures on South Africa, it is necessary to assess the effect
that they may have on our internal policies. Clearly we cannot continue for ever to swim against the tide; but this statement is only a generality and it would be a dangerous error
to think that external disapproval alone is about to cause
the fall of the Nationalist government. There are people,
both in and outside South Africa, who do in fact pin their
hopes on this assumption, but events are likely to prove
them wrong. For it must be clearly understood that threats
from outside are not resented only by the Nationalist Party
and its supporters: the broad mass of white South Africans
react against them. And white South Africans are both
powerful and tough. They believe with justification that a
good deal of the hostility towards South Africa is unreasonable and, as has been shown, has an ulterior motive.
This colours their attitude to what is reasonable and con-
structive, and there is little doubt that they would go to

great lengths to resist what they—rightly or wrongly—regard as unjustifiable pressure.

Certain overseas critics are capable of influencing South African policies. They are those whose image in the Union is one of friendship and helpfulness. The ancient metaphor of the palm tree is apposite here: those who are understood to wish us well may persuade South Africa to bend before the wind and preserve herself; those who seem to be hostile to us are likely to evoke a reaction of rigidity which will break rather than bend.

VIII

SOUTH AFRICA'S SICKNESS: SYMPTOMS, CAUSE AND TREATMENT

Enough has already been said about the signs of strain which have appeared in the South African society. Everyone knows that there is something wrong; and this fact is highlighted by a comparison of the general opinion of South Africa in, say, 1945 and 1960. Until the end of the war South Africa was regarded as a stable and reasonably progressive country. Now people outside and even inside the Union tend to take an almost opposite view. Before attempting to prescribe the remedy for South Africa's disease one must establish its nature as accurately as possible.

There are those who take a simple view of the whole matter and aver that all the trouble is due to the accession to power of the Nationalists in 1948. Now there is no doubt at all that many of the government's actions have inflamed race tensions, undermined economic confidence and damaged our overseas reputation. But to suggest that this is the whole of the story is surely unrealistic. Can anyone really believe that the Africans today would be content with even the milder form of pass laws and influx control which we knew in 1948? Or that, with a different government in power, they would accept the denial of trade union rights? Is it realistic to think that the Indians would now accept what they—albeit wrongly—rejected in 1946, namely a limited indirect representation in Parliament? Is it likely that the Coloured people would accept the denial of the vote to their womenfolk or their brothers in the Northern Provinces? And can anyone envisage world opinion remaining silent about a policy of White Leadership, even with a substantial admixture of Justice? The conclusion is clear. South Africa's difficulties are due to the fact that the system of government is now out of accord with the facts of power, partly because the system has changed but largely because the facts have changed. One has only to think of the map of Africa in 1948 and now to see how very rapid is the march of history. It has left our system of government far behind.

None of this is intended as criticism of the pre-1948 governments of South Africa. No doubt they had many faults, but it is worth re-emphasising that they did maintain a fair degree of stability and progress. What we have to determine are the reasons why that state of affairs has changed so radically. Now we have postulated that stability depends on two things: the political maturity of the citizenry and the nature of the social forces and whether they are compatible with the system of government. Clearly, the maturity of the South African people has not diminished. On the contrary—and let this be said to the credit of the government—education, income and social services among the under-privileged have all increased, though perhaps not improved, over the last twelve years; while industrialisation, urbanisation and sheer political experience have all progressed rapidly. So the apparent instability must be due to alterations in the social forces. And this is precisely what our survey shows.

Before 1948, Afrikaner nationalism was far more united and zealous than it is now. True, it lacked the strength which comes from success; but it had a far clearer vision of its aims than it has today. Among other white South Africans there were progressive thinkers, but the course of history had not thrust them forward as it has now: on the whole a comfortable conservatism prevailed. The non-whites themselves were virtually insignificant as a political force; and in so far as they had any power it was given some recognition by a government which sincerely tried to keep in touch with them. The national institutions did not inter-fere; the businessmen were content; economic forces were given fairly free play. In short, there was no social force

seriously distorting the system of government. Now all this
has changed, and an entirely new balance of forces has
emerged.

It is correct, though it is not the whole of the story, to say
that African nationalism has been enormously strengthened,
as a result of rapid economic integration, developments in
Africa and changed world attitudes. It is much stronger
than it was, and it is making urgent demands. And if
African nationalism were the only force opposing Afrikaner
nationalism, there would be little chance indeed of its
demands being met, even in part, without a long, bitter,
destructive struggle. Further, if the positions were reversed,
and African nationalism given free rein, it is virtually certain that some of its edicts would be implacably and
violently resisted. It is this sort of analysis of the position
which makes people despondent about South Africa's future,
and drives them, if they are South Africans, either to
preach partition or emigrate; or if they are not South
Africans, to lose their confidence in the Union's future. It is
observed, and rightly observed, that neither a government
of white supremacists nor one of black supremacists would
be able to govern with any success; and because this is so
the pessimists assume that there cannot be a future for
South Africa. In doing so they overlook two considerations
which must be conceded as having at least some validity.
The first is that the extremism of nationalist movements
almost always tends to moderate as more and more of their
demands are met. We have tried to show that this is already
beginning to happen among at least some influential
sections of the Afrikaner nationalists. It is not, of course,
happening to African nationalism now, because none of its
demands are being met, but that is not to say that it could
not happen, and those who have had some personal contact
with major African leaders are often optimistic about this
possibility. In other words, even if these two extreme
dynamic forces were the only ones in the field, compromise
should not be dismissed as utterly impossible.

The second consideration is even more important. There are, as we have seen, a number of other forces at work, and none of them is to be dismissed as insignificant. Of course they differ in direction: for example, the force of world opinion, as seen from within South Africa at any rate, is very near to full support for black nationalism, while to many people overseas all white South Africans look like white supremacists. Yet no one will deny that all the forces referred to in earlier chapters act in a direction intermediate between that of the two nationalisms. In a word, they are forces of compromise. Since Afrikaner nationalism is today in the ascendancy they all operate to oppose or at least to restrain it; but it is not fanciful to presume that if black nationalism were the dominant sectional force, these same groups and interests would be restraining it and defending the legitimate interests of the white people. And the minorities, white and brown, more especially when backed by so many of the intellectual, ecclesiastical and financial leaders of the community, constitute a formidable force.

When all is said and done, what is either impossible or disreputable about a compromise agreement in South Africa? Forces which seemed to be implacably opposed in other places and at other times have been reconciled in this way. There is scarcely a nation in the world where different interests do not each defer some of their aspirations for the sake of maintaining a stable society. Why should South Africans not do the same? It is at this point that the first of the two requirements we set for stability becomes important —the political maturity of the people. Now it is fashionable for the Jeremiahs in South Africa to cry 'Congo!', the implication being that since irreconcilable forces smashed that society, they will do so in the Union too. To say this is to ignore completely the facts in the two countries. As has been pointed out, the population of the Congo is largely illiterate and heathen and has no experience of government other than tribalism or colonial rule. The Congo is not the only country in Africa and Asia where Western democracy has failed to take root. Indeed it can be cogently argued that Western democracy is the one sort of government that cannot work in such countries. They can be governed either by external powers or by internal dictatorships, but in any case only by *force majeure*. This is by no means true of South Africa. Not only the white and brown people, but very large numbers of the black citizens of the Union are fully aware of the necessity to preserve ordered democratic government, even at considerable cost in sacrifice of aspirations.

It cannot be too often repeated that the black South African has become more westernised than his counterpart elsewhere—not because he is inherently superior, but simply because he has had so much more contact with Western civilisation. A very experienced African administrator, an Englishman, once observed that what the peoples of Africa want is civilisation, and that the best way of giving it to them is to present them with the largest possible front of contact with it. These conditions, he pointed out, are provided in South Africa to a far greater degree than anywhere else, and therefore, despite the alarming symptoms discernible at present, South Africa's chance of ultimate stability should be better than those of other territories. Where the African could not get civilisation, this administrator added, he would relapse into atavism. Events in various parts of Africa have proved him right; and the continued adherence of many Africans here to Western standards in the face of all their difficulties is again supporting his opinion.

But the fact that the African leaders want order and democracy is not merely due to a theoretical attachment to a political concept. They know that they require the economic partnership of the white man in order to maintain and improve standards; and similarly no white man really believes in or envisages a South Africa without black labour. Of course there are politicians, both white and black, who are fond of striking attitudes, who say that in order to achieve apartheid or universal suffrage as the case may be they will sacrifice every other desirable thing in life. There is little, however, in the behaviour of their followers that encourages one to believe them. All the evidence is to the contrary: it suggests that economic necessity easily overcomes these political attitudes. It suggests, in short, that in practice the most intransigent white and the hastiest black man can agree on the necessity for some form of economic partnership. Apart from the economic incentive to co-operation, moreover, the simple fact has to be borne in mind that there is a nice balance of power between white and black in South Africa. It is not Ghana or Guinea, Indonesia or Burma, where nationalist aspirations can be realised simply by packing off 'home' a handful of white officials, entrepreneurs and technicians. Equally, as has been emphasised again and again, white supremacy simply cannot be maintained in the Union except for a short time, and then only at the expense of grave unrest and severe restrictions on civil liberties. In other words, the stage is rapidly approaching, if it has not already arrived, at which the sheer instinct of self-preservation will compel co-operation between black and white. As Mr. Harry Oppenheimer once said, 'The real choice before South Africans is the choice whether, living together as they must, the different races are going to quarrel or co-operate.'

This is precisely true, and it would be a hard judgment indeed to believe that South Africans will deliberately enter a future of constant strife. Instead, a review of the present position suggests that they will find a new line of government which will correspond to the altered facts of power, and which will be found somewhere along the line advocated by the forces of compromise, between the two extreme sectional nationalisms.

IX

THE RESULTANT FORCE

It is time now to return to our argument that a determination of the composite effect of all the social forces operating in South Africa can offer a rough guide to political wisdom. Naturally, no precise calculation of the resultant force can be made because we have no accurate method of measuring the primary forces. One can only estimate; and the best estimate one can make is that the resultant force will be found somewhere between the extremes, and rather nearer to African aspirations than to the white supremacy line. In other words, any government attempting to maintain white supremacy will soon run into daunting difficulties, which will eventually become insuperable and demand that the system be so altered as to satisfy African aspirations at least in some respects. Inadequate steps in this direction will at best only ameliorate the difficulties of government, and may even be summarily rejected by people who refuse to believe that half a loaf is better than no bread at all. Equally, of course, government on the basis sought by the African nationalists would be out of accord with the facts of power and would be made impossible by the resistance of the whites and perhaps of others.

Among the white people in the Union there are essentially three schools of thought on the race problem: the planners of a partitioned society, the planners of an integrated society, and those who prefer not to plan at all. Our reasons for rejecting the partition plan have been given; but let it now be said that it is at any rate a definable logical concept which is capable of being logically dealt with. One is in far greater difficulty in commenting on the *laissez-faire* approach, because it is so difficult to define a shadow. Essentially it is the reaction of people—very many people—who have perceived dimly that South African society requires pretty radical reform, but who, because of half-hidden fear, or self-satisfaction, or intellectual laziness or habituation to the concepts of a dead era, simply do not want to face squarely up to the problem and decide what action it demands. Accordingly they have developed the sort of approach which makes no changes until these are forced upon them by events, and then just the very minimum change which in their view can be got away with. Now in other spheres than politics, and perhaps also in politics in countries whose problems are of a different sort, there may be something to be said for this; but in South Africa, where the problem is one of human relationships and is heavily charged with emotion, it is dangerous. For the professed reform, being limited, tardy and reluctant, is too often seen by those who are to benefit from it as a contemptuously thrown sop rather than a genuine effort at co-operation. Even though it might have been of value, it is then rejected, and often the end result is more militancy, greater demands and an exacerbation of the tension between government and governed. In the earlier days of Union, before racial tensions had developed, a *laissez-faire* approach must have seemed more attractive than it does now. Unfortunately however—and this is the other inherent fault of such an attitude—the ruling whites, aware of no urgent demand for reforms in the system, made no changes of any importance whatever, and in consequence the tensions arose and the day when *laissez-faire* might have offered any hope at all passed for ever. All this was succinctly summed up by the Hon. H. G. Lawrence, the distinguished opposition parliamentarian, in the Latin saying *Bis dat qui cito dat*. In the nineteen-sixties, a policy of edging slowly towards what is politically right will not do: the politically right course must be clearly determined and fearlessly taken.

What should that course be? It is not the function of this work to set out a complete political policy in all its detail, but it would be cowardly not to give an indication of the practical steps that seem wise. We have said that the proper line will be found between what African nationalism demands and what white supremacy insists on. Briefly, African nationalism asks for universal adult suffrage with unrestrained power for the majority, and the breaking down of all statutory racial barriers in every sphere. White supremacy insists upon white political control at least wherever white men live, the protection of white economic standards, and the protection of the white man's social exclusiveness. The intermediate forces in South Africa take up intermediate positions, siding in some matters with the white supremacists and in some with African aspirations.

In the political field the white demand for white control for an indefinite period into the future is manifestly unjust and unreasonable. This is not to say that white people should not be in a majority on the voters' rolls and in Parliament for a long time yet, provided they can achieve this on their merit. But the moment a political party says—as most white parties do in South Africa—that as a matter of policy it will maintain white control, this implies that it will load the voters' roll on a racial basis or adapt some other discriminatory methods of ensuring that the white man retains his dominance even when he does not deserve it on merit.

Now it is clear that no programme whatever which includes this sort of provision can have the faintest hope of acceptance; because when a party says: 'It is our policy to maintain white political control', they are in effect saying to the blacks: 'It is our policy to treat you as inherently inferior beings.' This no black man can accept. In other words, the least that the white man must do is to adopt a policy which will give the black man a majority in Parliament if and when he deserves it. This means a qualified franchise, a multiple vote (really another adaptation of the same principle) or some other franchise system which is not racially discriminatory.

Of course the Africans, while seeing the qualified franchise as a great step forward in white thinking, would for the most part prefer universal adult suffrage. Many African leaders are aware of the dangers of mob exploitation which this system can involve; but they point out that it is now in general use in Western countries and advocated by the United Nations; they add that universal adult suffrage for whites was introduced in South Africa in 1931, and accepted by all parties; and in short they can see no motive other than racialism for withholding it from all races in the Union today.

As against this, white South Africans are almost unanimous in rejecting the suggestion—and many Coloured people and not a few Indians agree with them. They say that, in Africa at any rate, there is a grave danger that universal adult suffrage leads not to democracy but to its denial. It is worth quoting at some length here from a document known as the 'Molteno Report'. The Molteno Commission was appointed by the Progressive Party of South Africa to recommend on constitution and franchise. It consisted entirely of men who in South Africa are called 'liberals'. Its white members were unanimous in supporting the passage which follows in regard to adult suffrage:

'On the non-White side of South African society we are aware that the demand is general, among the politically conscious elements, for adult suffrage. This demand is due not only to a rational desire to protect the interests of the masses against the forces of exploitation and racial discrimination, such as have dominated South Africa throughout its past, but also to an identification of adult suffrage with a status of human dignity and self-respect. In this respect non-White South Africa is naturally affected by the ideology that has inspired the national liberation of the colonial peoples of Asia and Africa since the war. For these peoples a system that in Europe and America has traditionally been regarded as a technique of government has become a mystique and a symbol.

'Whilst fully understanding this attitude, we are bound to point out that it bears no necessary relation to personal freedom, the rule of law, ordered progress, or any of the other values that Western democracy was conceived in order to foster. Its inspiration is rather non-White nationalism, which, like all nationalisms, is ultimately totalitarian in its logical outcome.

'A modern nationalist mass movement naturally rejects voting qualifications that seek to enfranchise the stable elements in society. For, to the nationalist, the vote is a weapon to be used by the masses at the behest of an enthusiastic leadership.

'In the newly-independent states of Asia and Africa this is all very well. If their peoples seek to reject the standards and values of Western democracy, this is at least their own affair, and indeed, in the process, they may well evolve systems of their own that suit their own circumstances better. In the circumstances of South Africa, however, with its considerable and developed White minority, non-White movements thus inspired can lead only to a racial clash with unpredictable consequences. For non-White nationalism, from its nature, must seek to dominate the White minority, just as White nationalism, from its nature, must and does seek to dominate the non-White majority. For White South Africans, therefore, the issue would not be merely surrender of their dominance over others but surrender of their own self-determination.

'This is something that no national or religious minority in a plural society has ever been prepared to do. Faced with such an issue White South Africa would fight, since all incentive to seek an agreed solution would be lacking, and even defeat could hardly have worse consequences than immediate surrender.'

These are the two sides of the argument in South Africa. There is one obvious line of compromise agreement. The African must accept something less than his universal adult suffrage; the white man must concede a future black majority. A franchise must be devised, based on non-discriminatory criteria, which will allow for the gradual growth of African influence as the Africans develop their abilities. As the passage from the Molteno Report shows, the insistence of African politicians on adult suffrage is based very largely on understandable emotional reactions. It is also, of course, based on the suspicion that any qualified suffrage would be used to deny them full opportunity and might be manipulated to prevent them from ever obtaining the black majority to which they aspire. Any proposal for a qualified suffrage must therefore be coupled with two undertakings: first that everything possible will be done to hasten the provision of universal education so as to bring the vote within the reach of all; and second that the qualifications themselves will be constitutionally entrenched so as to prevent gerrymandering.

Just as the bulk of the Africans are suspicious of the qualified franchise because they fear it will deny them their rights, so are the bulk of whites, for precisely the opposite reason. In passing it may be observed that this probably shows that it is the right compromise. The white fear, put shortly, is that the moment the Africans do gain a majority in Parliament they will use it to discriminate against the whites and to make them an oppressed minority. Tragically, reactionary white politicians have become expert in encouraging this fear with cries of 'Congo' and the like. However, the fact that the fear is artificially whipped up does not mean that it is without foundation; and it is surely reasonable that the whites should demand the right to maintain their own standards and way of life provided that this can be done without injustice or unfairness to other groups. This, together with the need for entrenching franchise qualifications, means that South Africa needs a different type of constitution from the flexible British type which obtains today. To a greater or lesser extent, most of the opposition groups in South Africa have at least toyed with the idea of constitutional reform: recently the Progressive Party has produced a comprehensive plan for a rigid

constitution, broadly speaking of the American type, which
would guarantee the rights of all individuals and groups in
South Africa. While this plan has been subjected to a good deal
of criticism from various sources, it may be fairly said that
there is not a great deal of principled opposition to the concept. Those who do not support it are sceptical rather than
hostile: the fact is of course that neither the white supremacists nor those who wish to see unchecked black majority
rule have any need of it. Yet logic as well as the experience
of other plural societies suggests that constitutional reform
is of the essence of any peaceful compromise solution.

Broadly speaking, then, a political programme based on a
qualified franchise and a protective constitution would give
to the black man the assurance that no bar would prevent
him from attaining power on his own merit; to the white
man the assurance that he would not be subjected to rule by
uncivilised people; and to all sections the assurance that the
constitution would stand above Parliament as the protector
of their rights.

In the economic sphere, the problem is perhaps somewhat
less difficult; though this is not to say that there is not a great
deal of wrong to be put right. Today, the African is subject
first to the pass law-influx control system which effectively
denies him the right to sell his labour in the highest market;
secondly to a denial of the right to belong to recognised
trade unions; thirdly to what is called the industrial colour
bar, which, though for the most part somewhat ill-defined,
makes it difficult if not quite impossible for him to rise out
of the categories of unskilled and semi-skilled labour; and
fourthly to tremendous difficulties in the way of his obtaining higher skills. The Coloured and Asian people are not
subject to the first two disabilities, and have lesser though
real difficulties in the other respects. All non-whites have
hanging over them the sword of Damocles which is called
job reservation: legislation which empowers the Minister of
Labour simply to lay down that certain work shall be done
by people of a particular race. Of course this reservation may

be in favour of any racial group: but the government's avowed purpose is to use it to 'protect the white worker'.

This apparatus exists because, as already stated, the white man, by and large, is determined to protect his economic standards. However, as virtually all the expert opinion available has shown, it is not necessary for that purpose; and indeed it is demonstrable that the effect of all these restrictions is to limit productivity, restrict the internal market and therefore retard the improvement of standards of all groups. It is very important here to note the opinions of the Trades Union Council, representing the largest organised group of white workers. It campaigns actively in favour of the right of Africans to join trade unions; it is opposed to the pass law system; it demands higher wages for African labour; it condemns job reservation and it stands for the extension of opportunity to all workers. Now the Trades Union Council is naturally concerned, and vitally concerned, with the maintenance of white economic standards—or, as it would prefer to say, with the maintenance of civilised labour standards. Its method of achieving this, however, is not restrictive legislation. It insists simply on the maintenance, through collective bargaining, of 'the rate for the job'—the principle of equal pay for equal work regardless of race, which makes it impossible for civilised standards to be undermined by the use of cheap labour from population groups with lower living standards. Naturally this policy only works satisfactorily when jobs are properly evaluated; but this, though important, is a matter of detail rather than principle.

It is not necessary to enumerate all the other authorities who agree with the above. One should, however, add the striking fact that employers' organisations agree almost exactly with the trade unions. This line of thinking offers what is essentially required in the economic sphere. The maintenance of 'the rate for the job', together with the liberal reforms outlined above, would lead to a situation in which white and black aspirations could be reconciled.

E

White opposition to the necessary reforms is still strong; but it is largely based on confusion of thought, and on prejudice deliberately fanned by reactionary politicians. A process of explanation and education will have to be gone through; but there is no reason why the various attitudes should not be reconciled in what is clearly the interest of all.

Far more difficult than the economic problem is that of reconciliation in the social sphere. For most of South Africa's history, social *mores* were determined by custom and convention rather than by legislation, and there grew up a system of racial segregation which, though never absolute, was very general in its application. As a result, separate residential areas, schools, amenities, transport facilities and so on became a feature of South African life. In recent years, and particularly since the Nationalists took office, this largely conventional system has been reinforced by a mass of legislation, whose effect has been to increase the degree of racial separation to some extent, and to inflame controversy about these matters alarmingly. After all, it is not only in South Africa that this has proved to be a difficult problem: the world press has kept us all informed of difficulties in the Southern States of America and elsewhere.

It is necessary to recognise that the bulk of white South Africans would violently oppose any forced social integration; it is relevant also to point out that animosity on this level between the various non-white groups is by no means unknown. But the existence of these strong feelings is of course no excuse for maintaining injustice. There is no reason why adult South Africans should not freely choose the company in which they wish to live their private lives, provided firstly that this does not involve real injustice and secondly that unnecessary friction is, so far as possible, avoided.

For a long time to come, at any rate, the number of white people prepared to share schools, swimming pools, cinemas or residential areas with non-whites will remain small. An attempt to force integration would unquestionably lead to grave disturbance—disturbance about an issue which is, after all, less vital to the well-being of South Africa than politics or economics—and it would almost certainly tend to stifle the cautious liberalism which many white South Africans are beginning to show in these other matters. For these reasons, the path of wisdom would seem to be the application where necessary in this sphere of the doctrine of 'Separate but Equal'. Now South African lawyers are well aware that this involves great difficulties. Nevertheless, it has proved workable elsewhere, at least for longish periods, and while it may mean great inconvenience it does not mean injustice in the sense of adverse discrimination against any group.

It must be appreciated that the application of the 'Separate but Equal' doctrine in regard to amenities and residential areas would represent a very great step forward from present South African practice. The existing law provides not merely for reservation of separate amenities, but for this to be done without any consideration at all of fairness or equity, and in fact the provision for non-whites of amenities on a substantially equal scale with those presently enjoyed by the whites would in itself be a very formidable task. It should also be understood that the advocates of 'Separate but Equal' facilities do not regard the principle of separation as sacrosanct, or indeed as a principle at all. It simply seems to be the wisest method in existing circumstances. As and when people are prepared to use the same amenities on a non-racial basis, arrangements should be made accordingly. Social arrangements should, so far as this is possible, reflect the wishes of the people concerned. Finally, it should be noted that certain of the restrictions now imposed on social contact are entirely unjustifiable and should simply be repealed. These include the prohibition of mixed marriages, the provision whereby people can be prevented from attending church services and the power the Minister has to stop mixed gatherings in clubs and other places. While it is felt that integration should not be forced, no one should be deprived of freedom of association.

Such would be a policy designed to make the system of government fit the facts of power. It represents a close approximation to what is conceived to be the resultant force in South Africa today. To appreciate its merit one may look at it again from the two extreme standpoints. The white supremacist would have to give up his power to dominate; but he would have a constitutional assurance that his rights were secure, and the knowledge that the voters were qualified people. He would retain his economic standards while sharing them with others. He would be free to lead his social life as he wished. The African would not get universal adult suffrage; but no one would be debarred from political opportunity on grounds of race. He would have to accept the governmental limitations of a rigid constitution; but his own rights would receive equal protection with those of other groups. Economic opportunity would be free; and, although there would still in practice be certain social barriers, these would exist only where they were demanded, and substantial equality of amenities would remove the stigma which is now attached to separation.

Above all, a policy of this sort would make it possible for every South African to realise his potential ability in every sphere and to live a full and unfettered life. This in turn is the prerequisite of a common patriotism which would lead our people to think as South Africans and as human beings rather than as members of racial groups. And in the long run it is only the extinction of racialism that can bring South Africa happiness and success.

X

DIFFICULTIES: ALTERNATIVES: CONCLUSION

In the state of tension which race relations have reached, it is hardly surprising that the compromise suggested here has more opponents than advocates; and even its most passionate supporters are fully aware that it will not be easy either to win the necessary support for it or to implement it once it is accepted. It is illuminating to examine the principal objections that are raised in various quarters, and to see what are the logical consequences of the various critical attitudes.

The most general criticism is simply that it will not win acceptance by either the black or the white masses, because the sacrifices it seeks from each are too great. This requires to be answered firstly by objective examination of these sacrifices, and secondly by a consideration of the alternatives. The Africans are asked to sacrifice their aim of universal adult suffrage. But they have not got that now; nor will they get it except, figuratively and even perhaps literally, over the dead bodies of the whites. And even if it were attained, it would certainly result in the flight from South Africa of much of the white capital and know-how which is essential to the standard of living of all groups. That white insistence on white domination should elicit from black men an answering demand for black domination regardless of cost is understandable, and thus while the whites demand racial suffrage the Africans may be expected to demand adult franchise. If, however, the white offer is, as here suggested, a qualified franchise plus a drive for universal education, which means the genuine opportunity for every citizen ultimately to acquire the vote, then the situation is quite different. To say 'all or nothing' when nothing of value is offered is one thing: to say it in the face of such an offer from the whites would be, from the black point of view, blindly unreasonable. For a white government or party offering these reforms would have at its disposal not only the enormous power of the state, but also a degree of moral authority which the present government lacks; and it is unlikely indeed that extreme black demands could be won against it except as a Pyrrhic victory after an almost totally destructive struggle. Therefore the so-called sacrifice asked for is largely illusory: it is the sacrifice of an unattainable aim in order to obtain something of the greatest value.

To at least an equal extent, the 'sacrifice' sought from the whites is illusory too. White men may differ as to their estimates of the length of time for which they can maintain domination in multi-racial South Africa, but none seriously believes it can be permanent. There are still some who think that partition can resolve the problem, but their numbers and their faith are dwindling fast. And if for purposes of argument separate development is admitted as a possibility, it would involve crippling economic sacrifice and the very real strategic danger of surrounding a tiny white state with a number of populous, underdeveloped black ones. The choice for the white man is whether to meet the black man now on reasonable terms or whether to see not only his dominance but his standards and way of life inevitably destroyed before very long. The 'sacrifice' he is asked to make is that of something which he must needs lose, and in return for it he can gain what he now lacks—the security of living at peace with his fellow-countrymen.

These arguments reveal the alternatives to a compromise. In either case, failure to co-operate leaves strife as the only alternative. If that strife does not destroy South Africa, then it will be fruitless, for the problem of reconciliation will remain to be solved. If it does, what is the point of it? And it is necessary to say again and again that these black and white forces are very evenly balanced: this is the peculiarity of the Union's situation. There is an argument that sooner or later black numbers must tell. But must they? Must the majority always win? Is it accepted that the world struggle of today will inevitably be won by the numbers of Russia and China? Or is that not just another situation where, since the consequences of strife are too awful to contemplate, the means of co-existence simply have to be found? The parallels between the world situation and that of South Africa are too obvious to need emphasis.

There is another alternative eagerly contemplated by some: that a solution will be imposed on the Union from outside, by the UN or some other international body. The difficulties encountered by the United Nations in the Congo suggest that this possibility should be accepted with considerable reserve; but the really important question is: what solution would be imposed? Many if not all of the objections mentioned above to anything other than a compromise solution would still apply. The external agency would simply find itself in the same dilemma as any South African government. The choice would be the same.

There are certain more specific objections to the sort of programme outlined here. One of great importance concerns the efficacy of proposed constitutional safeguards. Critics hold that a constitution is only a piece of paper and would very probably be ignored at one of two foreseeable times in the future. The likely result of a qualified franchise would be a white majority in Parliament initially, with a gradual increase of non-white representation to the point where it became numerically superior. Now it is argued that either the whites, rather than concede the black majority, would stage some sort of unconstitutional *coup d'état* to prevent its coming into being; or the Africans, at the moment of gaining a majority, would sweep aside the entrenchments and either institute immediate adult suffrage or go further and discriminate actively against other groups. The answer to these suggestions is that either of these events might take place; but either would be a revolution, with all the potential consequences that that entails. Nobody can legislate against a revolution. The question one must ask is whether a revolution is a greater danger in the present South African situation or in the sort of future one that has been envisaged; and to this the answer must be that it is far more likely now. In any case, a *coup d'état* by whites would simply be an attempt to perpetuate the white domination which is now breaking down, while a black *coup d'état* would not be essentially different because it was backed by a majority of one in Parliament, if the constitution were rigid. It would involve all the dangers that an attempted revolution now would invite, with the additional factor that it would probably be far less sympathetically viewed from outside South Africa. You do not need a parliamentary majority to stage a revolution. What is important is that revolutions can only be prevented if the population generally assents to the constitution, and South Africa's task is to make this possible.

The next objection raised refers to a difficulty which is common to all developing countries. Unless economic standards can be steadily raised, stable government may well prove impossible. Indeed the very fact of offering political rights and economic opportunity to people at present under-privileged may raise their expectations and thus make this need more urgent. This is a real problem, but almost certainly less difficult in South Africa than elsewhere. First, our economic position, as has been shown, is relatively very strong indeed. Furthermore, our present failure to go ahead faster than we do is due primarily to two factors: inefficient use of labour due to racial restrictions and lack of investment confidence due mainly to fear of racial clashes. Now the implementation of the programme advocated in these pages would rapidly overcome the first and go a long way towards reversing the latter. And it is to be remembered that in South Africa the infrastructure of economic development is virtually complete. We could profit rapidly and substantially from an improvement in conditions. Thus there is every reason to suppose that the economic conditions for political progress would in fact exist.

The proposal to open up free economic opportunity while

maintaining a qualified franchise is suspect in some quarters on the ground that in fact the whites intend to cling to economic privilege unless and until the non-whites can by majority vote force them to concede it. A hundred or even twenty-five years ago this sort of argument had much to support it; but in the modern world and by South Africa's economic leaders at any rate it has been realised that the prosperity of the privileged depends upon rising standards for the under-privileged. The concept of the affluent society is here to stay. Indeed the rising, though still tragically low, economic standards of our non-whites constitute one of the main factors which makes their political advancement inevitable.

Finally, it is suggested by some critics that economic and political integration are bound to be followed by social integration which will bring race friction and 'make South Africa one huge Little Rock'. This is indeed a danger: the process of accustoming South Africans of various groups to contact with each other will be long and difficult. As has been indicated, this is the sphere in which it seems wise to proceed slowly and carefully. Financially, too, the provision of separate but equal facilities where these are required will mean considerable cost, but this must be borne. It will in any case be trivial compared to the cost of partition. Then there is the purely legal problem. The United States Supreme Court judgment that separate facilities in education are inherently unequal is frequently quoted, and some future South African Court could of course make a similar ruling. But it needs to be borne in mind that the American ruling referred only to education, and that even in that field the Courts had previously upheld the doctrine of separation with equality for some fifty years. It is not unreasonable that South Africans should ask for time to work out these relationships in a manner acceptable to all groups.

Such are the criticisms of those who oppose our solution. Among them as well as among those who support it, the question is constantly asked: Have we time for these reforms? South Africans abroad are constantly asked to give figures. Will our society survive for twenty years, or ten, or five or two? In this over-simplified form the question cannot be answered. If it asks how much time there is before a race clash, the answer is: none at all. For, tragically, race clashes are already occurring. But if the question is how much time there is before the society destroys itself utterly, then there is always time this side of the grave. The whole theme of this work has been that a strain is building up because the system of government has got out of touch with the facts; that for this reason the forces are building up which will compel an agreed solution; and that it is possible within limits to see what the agreed solution must be. Nowhere has it been suggested that South Africa will not have to endure more trouble, more disturbance, more suffering: only that the light is visible at the end of the tunnel. Certainly it is true that the need for reform is growing more urgent by the day; but that very fact means that reform is not becoming impossible.

No doubt the programme for co-operation which has been set out has its imperfections. But again one must stress the need to consider the alternatives, or lack of them. The faith of those who believe in this programme has been stated in characteristic terms by their leader, Dr. Jan Steytler, who says: 'In the end South Africa will be governed in this way—because there is no other way that South Africa can be governed.'

In answer, the cynics say that Dr. Steytler's faith is starry-eyed, his optimism naïve. But the faith that animates him and those who think as he does is not just a faith in South Africa: it is a faith in the human being and a faith in civilisation. If one believes that civilised human beings would rather co-operate than quarrel, would rather be governed constitutionally than by *force majeure*, then this programme has every chance of implementation in South Africa.

Two paradoxical facts stand out from this or any other

work on South Africa's problems. When all factors are taken into account, the South African situation is unique. On the other hand it is in very many respects a microcosm of the world situation. That is why it is important to the world that South Africans should find a solution; and important, too, to South Africans that that solution should be shown to the world. Long ago, on the eve of Union in 1908, a great South African perceived this with prophetic insight. She was Olive Schreiner, and she wrote:

'Every great nation of the past or present has contributed something to the sum total of things beautiful, good, or useful, possessed by humanity: therein largely lies its greatness. We in South Africa can never hope exactly to repeat the records of the past. We can never hope, like Greece, to give to the world its noblest plastic art; we can never hope, like Rome, to shape the legal institutions of half the world; the chief glory of England, that wherever she goes, whether she will or not, and even against her will, she spreads broadcast among the nations the seeds of self-governing institutions—may never be ours. But the great national parts are not exhausted; and there lies before us in South Africa a part as great and inspiring as any which any nation has ever been called upon to play—if we are strong enough to grasp it.

The problem of the twentieth century will not be a repetition of those of the nineteenth or those which went before it. The walls dividing continents are breaking down; everywhere European, Asiatic and African will interlard. The world on which the twenty-first century will open its eyes will be one widely different from that which the twentieth sees at its awaking. And the problem which this century will have to solve is the accomplishment of this interaction of distinct human varieties on the largest and most beneficent lines, making for the development of humanity as a whole, and carried out in a manner consonant with modern ideals and modern social wants. It will not always be the European who forms the upper layer; but in its essentials the problem will be everywhere the same.

'We in South Africa are one of the first peoples in the modern world, and under the new moral and material conditions of civilisation, to be brought face to face with this problem in its acutest form. On our power to solve it regally and heroically depends our greatness. If it be possible for us out of our great complex body of humanity (its parts possibly remaining racially distinct for centuries) to raise up a free, intelligent, harmonious nation, each part acting with and for the benefit of the others, then we shall have played a part as great as that of any nation in the world's record. And as we today turn our eyes towards Greece or Rome or England for models in those things wherein they have excelled, nations in the future, whatever their dominant class may be, will be compelled to turn their eyes towards us and follow our lead, saying, "Hers was the first and true solution of the problem".'[1]

[1] Olive Schreiner *Closer Union* (Constitutional Reform Association, Cape Town, 1960).

POSTSCRIPT

This work was about to go to press when Dr. Verwoerd withdrew South Africa's application to remain a member of the Commonwealth. The short-term situation remains confused: what is important is to try to assess the long-range effects of this development on the forces operating in multi-racial South Africa.

Commonwealth membership has acted as a moderating influence in our affairs. Afrikaner nationalism has been to some extent restrained by the wish of many of its supporters to keep the Commonwealth link, while world hostility towards the Union has been tempered by the fact of our membership.

These brakes are now off. Isolation will be likely to lead to a tightening-up of government measures to retain authority, and one must expect world repercussions. Further, militant black nationalists feel encouraged to press their demands with renewed energy in the belief that the world is behind them. Our future relationships with the U.N. are now also in doubt. If we do retain our membership we must expect even more hostility than that we have met in the past.

There are those who welcome all this in the belief that the crisis had better come sooner than later. In the long run, the clash of forces may well produce the same total effect. But the tribulation in store for us will be more acute, and the danger of irreparable damage greater.

The task of the moderate in South Africa is even heavier than it was before.